Easy Air
Fryer Cookbook 2021

Enjoy all the Flavor of Deep Fried with an Easy
Guide, Including Healthy Recipes and Affordable
Homemade Meals

Martine Haley

Table of Contents

—

3

INTRODUCTION

An air fryer is a kitchen appliance designed to deliver a tasty, crispy, golden-brown morsel of food without the use of oil or other cooking fats. It uses hot air instead of oil or other cooking fats to cook food quickly and evenly.

The air fryer can be used for making fried chips in addition to other foods.

There are several varieties of air fryers. One of the main categories is made up of countertop air fryers designed for individual use in the kitchen. These models sit on the worktop or counter top and feature a basket that sits on a wire rack. This forms the base that holds hot air that cooks food as it passes through it.

air fryer's air fryers are designed to help you make healthy and filling meals. Our electric fryers are perfect for people who want fresh, homemade fries without all of the fat. Our air fryer features a light-weight aluminum design that lets you move the appliance from room to room without worry. Each air fryer is also equipped with a thermostat, making it easy to adjust the temperature as needed.

An air fryer is an appliance that cooks food using high-speed air circulation. It is a perfect alternative to deep frying, baking or roasting, and works great for cooking fast and healthy meals.

How Does an Air Fryer Work?

The fan draws warm air from the bottom of the chamber, which rises and cools as it circulates. The food is then placed in the middle of the basket, and the fan circulates air around it, cooking it all at once. Food cooks faster than if you fried it in oil or baked it in an oven. The food doesn't become soggy like fried food does, either. Because the air circulates around the food rather than through it, you can use much less oil in your Air Fryer. Best of all, since no oil is being used for cooking, there's much less of an environmental impact!

What Types of Air Fryers are Available?

Air fryers come in a variety of sizes as well as different colors and designs. You may find one that has a View Master-like chrome trim or one with a retro design pattern that blends easily into your décor. Some Air fryers are as small as a rice cooker while others can be used to make large batches of French fries with recipes you create on your tablet! Some Air Fryer models have "smart" features that allow you to cook multiple foods at the same time; others have timers so you can automatically set them for particular times during the day. All versions sterilize their own cooking plates by running them through a clean cycle between batches!

When you are looking for a new air fryer, you should take a look at air fryer Cookware. We have all of the features you are looking for in an air fryer, including built in racks that will allow you to cook a full size meal for your family. We also have a variety of accessories that will give you an even better cooking experience.

We are proud to introduce air fryer Cookware, the premier brand in air fryers. You can rest assured that we only use the best materials to ensure our products will work for years to come. Our air fryers feature built-in racks, so you can cook a full-size meal at once. They also include an adjustable thermostat that ranges from 120 to 500 degrees Fahrenheit.

Whether you are looking to impress your family with gourmet French fries or just want to make your favorite chicken drumsticks and vegetables, air fryer Cookware has everything you need. Every item has been carefully tested to ensure safe and responsible use. All of our products carry a One Year Limited Manufacturer Warranty, so you can be confident that they will serve your needs well.

Squash and Pork Chops

Preparation Time: 10 minutes

Cooking Time: 40 minutes

Servings: 3

Ingredients:

- 40 oz pork, ground
- 1 medium-sized squash, cut into eighths
- 4 tbsp. dried sage
- 2 tbsp. clarified and unsalted butter
- 2 teaspoons dried thyme
- 2 teaspoons ground cinnamon
- 1 cup of fish broth
- 1 teaspoon of salt
- 1 teaspoon pepper

Directions:

1. Fix your Air fryer to sauté mode and melt the unsalted butter or use the skillet to melt the butter and then pour to your Air fryer.
2. Combine the salt, pepper, dried thyme, sage and cinnamonin a bowl. Season the pork with the spices mix. Form the pork chops. Add the chops into Air fryer.
3. Then, add in the squash and pour in the fish broth.

4. Make sure to lock the lid and cook on high pressure for 40 minutes.
5. Quick-release the pressure and transfer the pork chops to a plate.
6. Mound the squash around the pork chops nicely and ladle up the sauce (if any) all over the chops. Serve it with the red or white wine.

Nutrition: Calories – 258 Protein – 59 g. Fat – 64 g. Carbs – 201 g.

Pork Belly in Wine

Preparation Time: 10 minutes

Cooking Time: 50 minutes

Servings: 3

Ingredients:

- 20 oz pork belly
- 1 cup of onions, peeled and chopped
- 1 cup of white wine
- 3 tablespoons avocado oil
- 4 garlic cloves, minced
- ¼ teaspoon red pepper flakes
- 3 teaspoons sesame seeds

Directions:

1. In a bowl, combine the belly, pepper, onions, tomato sauce, garlic, oil, pepper flakes and sesame seeds and toss well. Pour the wine and marinate the pork for a couple of hours at room temperature or place in the fridge overnight. Add it to your air fryer and close the lid to cook on a HIGH pressure for around 40 minutes.

2. Open the lid and place the pork on the cutting board and slice it.

3. Return the pork to the air fryer and Put the air fryerto sauté mode.

4. Cook the pork for 10 minutes and portion it into three plates and dollop each plate with some sesame seeds.

Nutrition: Calories – 223 Protein – 42 g. Fat – 48 g. Carbs – 189 g.

Pork Meat and Pumpkin

Preparation Time: 10 minutes

Cooking Time: 55 minutes

Servings: 3

Ingredients:

- 2 pieces of ½ inch thick bone-in pork loin or rib
- 1 medium pumpkin, peeled and diced
- 4 tablespoons dried sage
- 2 tablespoons clarified and unsalted butter
- 2 teaspoons dried thyme
- 2 teaspoons ground cinnamon
- 1 cup of chicken broth
- 1 teaspoon of salt
- 1 teaspoon pepper

Directions:

1. Fix your Air fryer to sauté mode and melt the unsalted butter or use the skillet to melt the butter and then pour it into your Air fryer.

2. Combine the salt, pepper, dried thyme, sage and cinnamonIn a bowl,. Season the pork meat with the spices mix and toss it in the unsalted butter to cook for 10 minutes.

3. Then, add in the pumpkin and pour in the chicken broth.

4. Make sure to lock the lid and cook on high pressure for 45 minutes.

5. Quick-release the pressure and transfer the pork to a plate.

6. Spoon the pumpkin around the pork nicely and ladle up the sauce (if any) all over the meat. Serve it with the cold beer.

Nutrition: Calories – 386 Protein – 77 g. Fat – 81 g. Carbs – 286 g.

Spicy Instant Pork with Peanuts

Preparation Time: 15 minutes

Cooking Time: 55 minutes

Servings: 4

Ingredients:

- 25 oz pork, ground
- ½ large onion, chopped
- 1 cup of peanuts
- 1 garlic clove, minced
- 1 bay leaf
- 2 ounces tomato sauce
- 1 tablespoon olives, pitted
- 1 tablespoon cilantro, chopped
- ½ cup of water
- 2 teaspoon chili powder
- Salt and pepper, to taste

Directions:

1. Preheat the oven to 240°-260°F and roast the peanuts in the oven for 10 minutes until crispy and then let it cool completely. Then grind the peanuts using a food processor or blender.

2. Marinate the pork in the salt, pepper and chili powder for a couple of hours at room temperature or place in the fridge overnight. Fix the Air fryer to

sauté mode and add in the pork. Break the pork meat into pieces and cook until browned.

3. Add in remaining ingredients and mix well.

4. Make sure to lock the lid and cook on HIGH pressure for 45 minutes.

5. Then portion the pork into four plates. Serve it with the salad and brown rice.

Nutrition: Calories – 381 Protein – 71 g. Fat – 78 g. Carbs – 282 g.

Sunday Pot Roast

Preparation Time: 20 minutes

Cooking Time: 1 hour and 20 minutes

Servings: 6-8

Ingredients:

- 2 tablespoons canola oil
- 1 (3-pound) beef chuck roast
- Kosher salt
- Freshly ground black pepper
- 1 large onion, halved and sliced
- 4 garlic cloves, minced
- 4 fresh thyme sprigs
- 1 bay leaf
- 1¾ cups or 1 (14.5-ounce) can beef broth
- 1 pound new potatoes, halved, no bigger than 1-inch pieces
- 4 to 5 large carrots, cut into ¾-inch pieces
- 3 large parsnips, cut into ¾-inch pieces

Directions:

1. To preheat the Air fryer, Choose Sauté on high heat. Add the oil.
2. Season the roast with salt and pepper. Once the pot is hot, brown the roast on all sides, 3 to 4 minutes per side. Transfer the meat to a plate.

3. Add the onion and cook for 3 to 5 minutes until starting to brown. Add the garlic, thyme, bay leaf, and broth. Scrape the bottom of the pot to deglaze the pan. Return the meat to the pot and secure the lid.

4. Select Manual or Pressure Cook and cook at high pressure for 1 hour.

5. Once cooking is done, use a quick release. Add the potatoes, carrots, and parsnips, submerging them in the cooking liquid.

6. Select Manual or Pressure Cook and cook at high heat for 10 minutes.

7. When cooking is complete, use a natural release for 10 minutes and then release any remaining steam.

8. The potatoes should be fork-tender and the meat should be falling apart. Serve topped with the juice.

Nutrition: Calories – 1011 Protein – 64 g. Fat – 26 g. Carbs – 32 g.

One-Pot Pasta Bolognese

Preparation Time: 10 minutes

Cooking Time: 5 minutes

Servings: 4

Ingredients:

- 1 tablespoon extra-virgin olive oil
- 12 ounces lean ground beef
- 1 large onion, chopped
- 3 garlic cloves, minced
- ½ cup dry red wine
- ½ teaspoon kosher salt, plus more for seasoning
- ¼ teaspoon red pepper flakes
- 1½ cups water
- 12 ounces uncooked penne pasta (with a 9to 13-minute cook time)
- 1 (28-ounce) can crushed tomatoes in purée or good tomato sauce
- ½ cup shredded mozzarella cheese

Directions

1. Heat up the Air fryer by choosing Sauté on high heat.
2. Wait 1 minute and then add the oil. Add the ground beef and use a wooden spoon or spatula to break up and stir as it cooks, about 3 minutes.

3. Once the meat is cooked, putin the onion and stir. Cook for 1 minute and add the garlic. Cook for 1 minute more.

4. Add the wine and rake off the bottom to deglaze the pan. Cook for 1 to 2 minutes, or once the alcohol smell has gone away.

5. Add the salt, red pepper flakes, and water and stir. Add the pasta and stir. Pour the tomatoes or tomato sauce over in an even layer, covering the pasta. Secure the lid.

6. Select Manual or Pressure Cook and cook at high pressure for 5 minutes

7. As soon as done cooking, use a quick release. Test the pasta. If it isn't quite done, Choose Sauté and simmer for another 1 to 2 minutes. Serve topped with mozzarella.

Nutrition: Calories – 596 Protein – 45 g. Fat – 4 g. Carbs – 68 g.

Five-Spice Boneless Beef Ribs

Preparation Time: 15 minutes

Cooking Time: 35 minutes

Servings: 6

Ingredients:

- 6 boneless beef short ribs, trimmed
- 2 teaspoons Chinese five-spice powder
- Kosher salt
- 2 tablespoons canola oil
- 4 garlic cloves, minced
- 1-inch piece fresh ginger, finely chopped
- 2 tablespoons rice wine vinegar
- ½ cup beef broth
- ¼ cup soy sauce
- ¼ cup raw sugar or brown sugar

Directions:

1. Preheat the oven to broil.
2. Coat the ribs with the five-spice powder and season with salt. Place on a baking sheet and broil them for 3 minutes on each side.
3. Preheat the Air fryer by selecting Sauté. Add the oil
4. Put the garlic and ginger and sauté for 2 minutes, until starting to brown. Add in the vinegar and cook for another minute. Select Cancel and add the

broth, soy sauce, and sugar and stir until the sugar dissolves. Add the ribs and secure the lid.

5. Select Manual or Pressure Cook and cook at high pressure for 35 minutes

6. Once done cooking, use a natural release. This will take about 15 minutes.

7. Take out the ribs and put them back on the baking sheet. Brush with the cooking liquid and broil again for 3 minutes per side to form a crust.

8. Meanwhile, Choose Sauté on high heat and reduce the sauce by up to half.

9. After broiling, brush the ribs on all sides with the sauce. Serve with extra sauce.

Nutrition: Calories – 247 Protein – 27 g. Fat – 2 g. Carbs – 10 g.

Corned Beef

Preparation Time: 5 minutes

Cooking Time: 1 hour and 30 minutes

Servings: 8

Ingredients:

- 1 (3½to 4-pound) flat-cut corned beef
- 1 (12-ounce) bottle beer (lager or pilsner is best)
- 2 cups chicken broth
- 1 onion, quartered
- 1 bay leaf
- Freshly ground black pepper

Directions:

1. Rinse the corned beef and pat dry. Cut off the extra fat, leaving a thin layer.

2. Place the corned beef in the Air fryer and cover with the beer and broth. Add the onion and bay leaf and season with pepper. Secure the lid.

3. Select Manual or Pressure Cook and cook at high pressure for 1½ hours.

4. Once done cooking, use a natural release. This will take 15 to 20 minutes.

5. Remove the meat using tongs, and let it rest a few minutes before slicing.

Nutrition: Calories – 388 Protein – 28 g. Fat – 0 g. Carbs – 3 g.

Oxtail Ragu

Preparation Time: 20 minutes

Cooking Time: 1 hour

Servings: 4

Ingredients:

- 2 tablespoons canola oil
- 12 (3-inch) oxtail pieces, rinsed and dried
- Kosher salt
- Freshly ground black pepper
- 2 tablespoons butter
- 1 onion, chopped
- 2 carrots, peeled and chopped
- 2 celery stalks, chopped
- ½ cup dry red wine
- 1 (28-ounce) can whole tomatoes, drained
- ½ cup beef broth or water
- Pinch red pepper flakes

Directions

1. Warm up the Air fryer by choosing Sauté on high heat. Add the oil.
2. Flavor the oxtails well with salt and pepper. Once the pot is hot, add half of the oxtails in a single layer. Cook for 4 minutes, or until browned. Flip and

repeat on the other side. Repeat with the rest of the oxtails and set aside.

3. Carefully drain all but 1 to 2 tablespoons of the fat.

4. Add the butter. Once melted, add the carrots,celery, and onion, Cook, stirring occasionally, for 2 minutes. Add the wine and scrape up any brown bits off the bottom of the pot. Cook for about 2 minutes, or until the smell of alcohol goes away.

5. Add the tomatoes, squishing them with your hands before dropping them into the pot. Add the broth and red pepper flakes. Flavor with salt and pepper and lock the lid.

6. Select Manual or Pressure Cook and cook at high pressure for 1 hour.

7. Once done cooking, use a natural release. This will take 15 to 20 minutes.

8. Remove the oxtails and carefully strip the meat off the bones. Put the meat back to the sauce and stir. Serve.

Nutrition: Calories – 621 Protein – 55 g. Fat – 13 g. Carbs – 15 g.

Lamb Curry

Preparation Time: 35 minutes

Cooking Time: 20 minutes

Servings: 4-6

Ingredients:

- 1½ pounds boneless lamb, trimmed of fat and cut into 1-inch cubes
- Kosher salt
- Freshly ground black pepper
- 1-inch piece fresh ginger, peeled and grated
- 4 garlic cloves, minced
- ⅓ cup plain yogurt
- 1 tablespoon butter
- 1 small onion, diced
- 2½ teaspoons garam masala
- ½ teaspoon turmeric
- 1 (14.5-ounce) can of tomatoes, diced, with juice
- Fresh cilantro, for garnish

Directions:

1. Season the lamb with salt and pepper. In a large bowl, combine the lamb, ginger, garlic, and yogurt. Let marinate for at least 30 minutes or up to 8 hours in the refrigerator.

2. Add the lamb and all of its liquid, along with the butter, onion, garam masala, turmeric, and the tomatoes with its juice to the Air fryer. Season with salt and pepper and stir. Secure the lid.

3. Select Manual or Pressure Cook and cook at high pressure for 20 minutes.

4. Once done cooking, use a natural release. If a thicker sauce is desired, Choose Sauté and cook on high heat until the sauce has thickened.

5. Top with fresh cilantro and serve.

Nutrition: Calories – 391 Protein – 51 g. Fat – 7 g. Carbs – 9 g.

Pulled Pork

Preparation Time: 5 minutes

Cooking Time: 45 minutes

Servings: 6-8

Ingredients:

- 1 (4-pound) boneless pork roast, trimmed of excess fat
- 3 packed tablespoons brown sugar
- 2 tablespoons chili powder
- 2 tablespoons smoked paprika
- 1 teaspoon ground cumin
- 1 teaspoon kosher salt
- ½ teaspoon freshly ground white pepper
- ¾ cup apple cider or water
- ½ cup apple cider vinegar
- ½ cup ketchup
- 6 to 8 soft hamburger buns

Directions:

1. Cut the pork roast against the grain into 4 equal pieces.
2. In a small bowl, combine the brown sugar, chili powder, paprika, cumin, salt, and pepper. Rub the pork roast until covered with the spice mixture.

3. Add the apple cider or water, vinegar, and ketchup to the Air fryer and stir. Add the spice-rubbed pork and secure the lid.
4. Select Manual or Pressure Cook and cook at high pressure for 45 minutes.
5. Once done cooking, select Cancel and use a natural release. This will take about 15 minutes
6. Move the pork to a plate and let it cool slightly. Shred with a fork, trimming off and discarding any extra fat.
7. Skim excess fat from the cooking liquid. Choose Sauté and simmer the sauce for about 20 minutes, or until it measures at the 2-cup line. Season with salt and pepper if needed.
8. Put half of the sauce to the pork and stir to combine. Serve on soft hamburger buns with more sauce.

Nutrition: Calories – 624 Protein – 84 g. Fat – 4 g. Carbs – 37 g.

One-Pot Beans, Sausage, and Greens

Preparation Time: 10 minutes

Cooking Time: 5 minutes

Servings: 4-6

Ingredients:

- 1 tablespoon extra-virgin olive oil
- 12 ounces Italian-style or hot sausage, without casing
- 1 medium yellow onion, chopped
- 3 garlic cloves, minced
- 1 large bunch collard greens, chopped
- 2 cans of pinto beans, drained and rinsed
- ½ cup chicken broth or water
- Kosher salt
- Freshly ground black pepper

Directions:

1. To preheat the Air fryer, select Sauté.
2. Once warm enough, add the oil followed by the sausage. Cook, breaking apart with a wooden spoon or spatula, until the sausage is browned and cooked through. Remove the sausage and save for later.
3. Put the onion to the pot and cook for 2 minutes. Put the garlic in and cook for 1 minute more, or until the onions are translucent.

4. Add the greens, beans, and broth, and season with salt and pepper. Stir. Secure the lid.

5. Select Manual or Pressure Cook and cook at high pressure for 5 minutes.

6. Once done cooking, select Cancel and use a quick release.

7. Add the sausage. Taste and adjust the seasoning. If you want less liquid, Choose Sauté on high heat and cook for up to 5 minutes.

Nutrition: Calories – 648 Protein – 37 g. Fat – 9 g. Carbs – 60 g.

Teriyaki Pork Loin

Preparation Time: 2 hours and 10 minutes

Cooking Time: 25 minutes

Servings: 4-6

Ingredients:

- 1 (2to 2½-pound) boneless pork loin roast, trimmed of excess fat
- ½ cup lower-sodium soy sauce
- ½ cup pineapple juice
- 3 tablespoons brown sugar
- 6 garlic cloves, minced, divided
- 1 heaping teaspoon grated fresh ginger
- 2 tablespoons canola oil
- 1 large red onion, cut into ⅛-inch slices
- 2 tablespoons rice wine vinegar

Directions:

1. In a large bowl or large resealable plastic bag, combine the pork, soy sauce, pineapple juice, brown sugar, 2 of the minced garlic cloves, and the grated ginger. Set aside in the refrigerator for at least 2 hours or overnight.

2. Choose Sauté on high heat on the Air fryer and add the oil.

3. Remove the roast from the marinade and let drain, reserving the marinade. Brown the roast in the oil on all sides, about 3 minutes per side. Transfer the meat to a plate.

4. With the pot still on Sauté, add the onion and cook, stirring frequently, for 3 minutes until starting to brown. Add the remaining cloves and cook for 1 minute more. Add the roast and the reserved marinade, adding a little water if needed to bring the total liquid to 1 cup. Secure the lid.

5. Select Manual or Pressure Cook and cook at high pressure for 25 minutes

6. Once done cooking, use a natural release. Test the pork for doneness—it should be at least 140°F in the center. Remove the roast and let it rest. Add the vinegar to the sauce.

7. Choose Sauté and simmer for 5 minutes to decrease the sauce.

8. Slice the meat then serve with sauce spooned over the top.

Nutrition: Calories – 485 Protein – 63 g. Fat – 3 g. Carbs – 20 g.

Easy Hawaiian-Style Pork

Preparation Time: 5 minutes

Cooking Time: 1 hour and 30 minutes

Servings: 8

Ingredients:

- 1 (5-pound) bone-in pork roast
- 1 onion, quartered
- 6 garlic cloves, minced
- 1½ tablespoons red Hawaiian coarse salt or 1 tablespoon red Hawaiian fine salt
- Freshly ground black pepper
- 1 cup water

Directions:

1. Cut the pork roast into thirds. Put it in the bottom of the Air fryer in a single layer.
2. Add the onion, garlic, and salt, and season with pepper. Add the water and secure the lid.
3. Select Manual or Pressure Cook and cook at high pressure for 1½ hours.
4. Once done cooking, select Cancel and use a natural pressure release. This will take 15 to 20 minutes.
5. Shred the pork and serve with the juice.

Nutrition: Calories – 536 Protein – 51 g. Fat – 13 g. Carbs – 2 g.

German Sausages with Peppers and Onions

Preparation Time: 12 minutes

Cooking Time: 10 minutes

Servings: 4

Ingredients:

- 2 tablespoons butter or canola oil
- 4 large German sausages, such as bratwurst
- 1 large onion, halved and cut into ¼-inch slices
- 1 green bell pepper, cut into ¼-inch rings
- 1 red bell pepper, cut into ¼-inch rings
- 1 (12-ounce) bottle German-style lager
- Kosher salt
- Freshly ground black pepper
- 4 hoagie rolls
- Good-quality mustard, for serving

Directions:

1. To preheat the Air fryer, select Sauté. Add the butter or oil.

2. Once hot, add the sausages. Brown them on both sides. This will take 5 to 10 minutes.

3. Remove the sausages and turn the heat to high. Add the onion and stir. Cook for 4 to 5 minutes until the onion starts to brown.

4. Add the peppers and lager and stir. Cook for 1 minute. Season with salt and pepper. Add the sausages and secure the lid.

5. Select Manual or Pressure Cook and cook at high pressure for 10 minutes

6. Once done cooking, use a natural release. Serve the sausages on hoagie rolls topped with the peppers and onions and mustard.

Nutrition: Calories – 624 Protein – 23 g. Fat – 13 g. Carbs – 57 g.

Beef Burgundy

Preparation Time: 10 minutes

Cooking Time: 35 minutes

Servings: 8

Ingredients:

- ¼ cup all-purpose flour
- 2 tablespoons extra-virgin olive oil
- 2 pounds beef chuck roast, cut into bite –size cubes
- 2 garlic cloves, minced
- 1 medium yellow onion, diced
- 1 teaspoon dried thyme
- 1 teaspoon fine sea salt
- ½ teaspoon freshly ground black pepper
- 1 cup red wine
- 1 tablespoon tomato paste
- 4 carrots, peeled and sliced (about 1 cup)

Directions:

1. Place the beef and flour in a zip-top bag. Seal the bag and then make sure the beef gets coated with the flour.
2. Choose Sauté and add the olive oil to the inner pot. Once the oil is warm enough, addthe flour-coated beef, garlic, onion, thyme, salt, and pepper; sauté for 3 minutes, stirring occasionally.

3. Press Cancel and pour in the wine. Using a wooden spoon, remove any browned bits stuck to the bottom of the pot. Add the tomato paste and carrots and stir to combine.

4. Secure the lid into place. Choose Pressure Cook or Manual; fix the pressure to High and the set to 30 minutes. Ensure the steam release knob is in the sealed position. Once done cooking, naturally release the pressure for 10 minutes, then quick release any remaining pressure.

5. Unlock and remove the lid. Serve immediately, or place the beef and sauce in an sealed container and refrigerate for up to 4 days or freeze for up to 2 months.

Nutrition: Calories – 307 Protein – 34 g. Fat – 11 g. Carbs – 12 g.

Beef Stroganoff With Spring Green Peas

Preparation Time: 15 minutes

Cooking Time: 20 minutes

Servings: 6

Ingredients:

- 2 tablespoons cornstarch
- ½ cup water
- 2 tablespoons extra-virgin olive oil
- 2 pounds sirloin steak, cut into strips
- 3 garlic cloves, minced
- 2 shallots, diced
- 2 cups button mushrooms, sliced
- 1 cup low-sodium beef broth
- 2 cups green peas (thawed if frozen)
- 2 tablespoons Dijon mustard
- ¼ cup chopped fresh dill
- ⅓ cup low-fat plain Greek yogurt
- Juice of 1 medium lemon

Directions:

1. In a bowl, create a slurry by whisking together the water andcornstarch. Reserve.

---

2. Choose Sauté and add the olive oil to the inner pot. Once the oil is hot, use tongs to place the beef strips into the pot. Cook the beef, stirring constantly, for 2 minutes or until it starts to brown. Add the garlic, shallots, and mushrooms and stir to combine.

3. Press Cancel and add the broth. Using a wooden spoon, remove any browned bits stuck to the bottom of the pot.

4. Lock the lid into place. Choose Pressure Cook or Manual; fix the pressure to High and the time to 10 minutes. Ensure the steam release knob is in the sealed position. Once done cooking, naturally release the pressure for 10 minutes, then quick release any remaining pressure.

5. Unlock and remove the lid. Select Sauté.

6. Add the peas, cornstarch slurry, and mustard and whisk to combine. Continue whisking for 2 more minutes or until the sauce starts to thicken. Press Cancel and stir in the dill, yogurt, and lemon juice.

7. Serve immediately, or place the stroganoff in an airtight container and refrigerate for up to 4 days.

Nutrition: Calories – 306 Protein – 39 g. Fat – 11 g. Carbs – 12 g.

Barbacoa Beef

Preparation Time: 10 minutes

Cooking Time: 35 minutes

Servings: 8

Ingredients:

- 2 tablespoons extra-virgin olive oil
- 2 garlic cloves, minced
- 1 medium yellow onion, diced
- 1 teaspoon ground cumin
- ½ teaspoon dried oregano
- 2 lbs beef chuck roast, sliced to 2-inch cubes
- ½ teaspoon chili powder
- 1 teaspoon fine sea salt
- ½ teaspoon freshly ground black pepper
- 1 cup low-sodium beef broth
- Juice of 2 limes
- 1 (4-ounce) can diced green chiles

Directions:

1. Choose Sauté and add the olive oil to the inner pot. Once the oil is warm enough, add the beef, garlic, onion, cumin, oregano, chili powder, salt, and pepper; sauté for 3 minutes, stirring occasionally.

2. Press Cancel and pour in the broth, lime juice, and green chiles. Using a wooden spoon, remove any browned bits stuck to the bottom of the pot.

3. Secure the lid into place. Choose Pressure Cook or Manual; fix the pressure to High and set to 30 minutes. Ensure the steam release knob is in the sealed position. Once done cooking, naturally release the pressure for 10 minutes, then quick release any remaining pressure.

4. Unlock and remove the lid. Stir the mixture. If you want to shred the beef, use two forks to pull apart each piece.

5. Serve immediately, or place the beef in a sealed container and refrigerate for up to 4 days or freeze for up to 2 months.

Nutrition: Calories – 256 Protein – 31 g. Fat – 4 g. Carbs – 3 g.

Pot Roast with Carrots and Potatoes

Preparation Time: 10 minutes

Cooking Time: 45 minutes

Servings: 6

Ingredients:

- 2 tablespoons extra-virgin olive oil
- 1 (2-pound) beef chuck roast
- 2 garlic cloves, minced
- 1 medium yellow onion, diced
- 2 cups low-sodium beef broth
- 1½ pounds medium red potatoes, quartered
- 4 large carrots, cut into 2-inch pieces
- ½ teaspoon dried oregano
- 2 teaspoons Worcestershire sauce
- 2 bay leaves
- 1 teaspoon fine sea salt
- ½ teaspoon freshly ground black pepper

Directions:

1. Choose Sauté and add the olive oil to the inner pot. Once the oil is hot enough, add the beef, garlic, and onion and cook for 3 minutes, turning the beef once so it browns on both sides.

2. Press Cancel and pour in the broth. Using a wooden spoon, remove any browned bits stuck to the bottom

of the pot. Add the carrots, potatoes, oregano, Worcestershire sauce, bay leaves, salt, and pepper; stir to combine.

3. Secure the lid into place. Choose Pressure Cook or Manual; fix the pressure toHigh and the time to 40 minutes. Ensure the steam release knob is in the sealed position. Once done cooking, naturally release the pressure for 10 minutes, then quick release any remaining pressure

4. Open the lid. Stir the ingredients. Use tongs to remove and get rid of the bay leaves. If you want to shred the beef, use tongs to transfer it to a cutting board and two forks to shred the meat. Return the meat to the pot.

5. Serve immediately, or place the pot roast in a sealed container and refrigerate for up to 4 days or freeze for up to 2 months.

Nutrition: Calories – 362 Protein – 34 g. Fat – 14 g. Carbs – 24 g.

Sloppy Joes

Preparation Time: 5 minutes

Cooking Time: 15 minutes

Servings: 8

Ingredients:

- 1 tablespoon extra-virgin olive oil
- 2 pounds 90% lean ground beef
- 1 teaspoon onion powder
- ½ teaspoon garlic powder
- 1 teaspoon chili powder
- 1 (16-ounce) can tomato purée
- ½ cup ketchup
- 2 tablespoons reduced-sodium soy sauce
- 1 tablespoon brown sugar
- Purple slaw, for garnish (optional)
- Fresh chopped parsley, for garnish (optional)

Directions:

1. Choose Sauté and add the olive oil to the inner pot. Once the oil is warm enough, addthe ground beef and cook for 3 minutes, using a spatula for crumbling the meat.

2. Press Cancel and add the onion powder, garlic powder, chili powder, tomato purée, ketchup, soy sauce, and brown sugar. Stir to combine.

3. Secure the lid into place. Choose Pressure Cook or Manual; fix the pressure toHigh and the time to 10 minutes. Ensure the steam release knob is in the sealed position. Once done cooking, release the pressure naturally for 10 minutes, then quick release the remaining pressure.

4. Open the lid. Stir the Sloppy Joe mixture to make sure it's well mixed.

5. Serve immediately garnished with purple slaw and parsley, if desired, or place the Sloppy Joes in an airtight container and refrigerate for up to 4 days or freeze for up to 2 months.

Nutrition: Calories – 246 Protein – 24 g. Fat – 12 g. Carbs – 7 g.

Broccoli Beef

Preparation Time: 20 minutes

Cooking Time: 19 minutes

Servings: 6

Ingredients:

- 2 tablespoons cornstarch
- ½ cup water
- 1 tablespoon extra-virgin olive oil
- 2 pounds flank steak, cut into ½-inch-thick slices
- 3 garlic cloves, minced
- ½ cup low-sodium beef broth
- ⅓ cup reduced-sodium soy sauce
- ¼ cup white wine vinegar
- 1 tablespoon brown sugar
- 2 teaspoons Sriracha sauce
- ¼ teaspoon ground ginger
- 1 pound broccoli florets, fresh or frozen (about 3½ cups)
- 4 scallions, sliced, for garnish

Directions:

1. In a bowl, create a slurry by mixing the water and cornstarch together. Set aside.
2. Choose Sauté and add the olive oil to the inner pot. Once the oil is warm enough, addthe steak and garlic

and sauté for 3 minutes, stirring once in a while so the beef starts to brown on both sides.

3. Press Cancel and add the broth. Using a wooden spoon, remove any browned bits stuck to the bottom of the pot. Add the soy sauce, vinegar, brown sugar, Sriracha, and ginger; stir to combine.

4. Secure the lid into place. Choose Pressure Cook or Manual; fix the pressure toHigh and the time to 8 minutes. Ensure the steam release knob is in the sealed position. Once done cooking, naturally release the pressure for 5 minutes, then quick release any remaining pressure.

5. Unlock and remove the lid. Add the broccoli florets.

6. Lock the lid into place again. Choose Pressure Cook or Manual; fix the pressure to High and the time to 1 minute. Ensure the steam release knob is in the sealed position. Once done cooking, quick release the pressure.

7. Open the lid. Choose Sauté. Use a slotted spoon to transfer the beef and broccoli to a serving plate.

8. Once the liquid is bubbling in the inner pot, whisk in the cornstarch slurry and let the sauce cook, uncovered, for 2 minutes or until it starts to thicken.

9. Return the beef and broccoli to the pot and stir to combine.

10. Serve the dish garnished with the scallions

Nutrition: Calories – 330 Protein – 35 g. Fat – 16 g. Carbs – 10 g.

Korean Beef Bowl

Preparation Time: 15 minutes

Cooking Time: 20 minutes

Servings: 6

Ingredients:

- 2 tablespoons cornstarch
- ½ cup water
- 1 tablespoon extra-virgin olive oil
- 2 pounds flank steak, sliced into ½-inch-thick strips
- 3 garlic cloves, minced
- ½ cup low-sodium beef broth
- ⅓ cup reduced-sodium soy sauce
- ¼ cup white wine vinegar
- 2 tablespoons honey
- 2 teaspoons Sriracha sauce
- ¼ teaspoon ground ginger
- 1 medium cucumber, sliced
- 2 red bell peppers, seeded and sliced
- 4 scallions, sliced

Directions:

1. In a bowl create a slurry by whisking the water and cornstarchtogether. Reserve.
2. Choose Sauté and add the olive oil to the inner pot. Once the oil is warm enough, addthe steak and garlic

---

and sauté for 3 minutes, stirring occasionally so the beef starts to brown on all sides.

3. Choose Cancel then add the broth. Using a wooden spoon, remove any browned bits stuck to the bottom of the pot. Add the vinegar, soy sauce, Sriracha,honey, and ginger; stir to combine.

4. Secure the lid into place. Choose Pressure Cook or Manual; fix the pressure toHigh and the time to 10 minutes. Ensure the steam release knob is in the sealed position. Once done cooking, release the pressure naturally for 5 minutes, then quick release any remaining pressure.

5. Unlock and remove the lid. Select Sauté. Use a slotted spoon to transfer the beef to a serving plate.

6. Once the liquid begins to bubble, whisk in the cornstarch slurry and let the sauce cook, uncovered, for 2 minutes or until it starts to thicken. Place the beef back to the pot and stir to combine.

7. Serve every bowl with a few slices of cucumber and red bell pepper and some sliced scallions on top.

Nutrition: Calories – 355 Protein – 36 g. Fat – 16 g. Carbs – 16 g.

Mongolian Beef And Broccoli

Preparation Time: 10 minutes

Cooking Time: 16 minutes

Servings: 6

Ingredients:

- 2 tablespoons cornstarch
- ½ cup water
- 2 tablespoons extra-virgin olive oil
- 1 medium yellow onion, chopped
- 2 pounds skirt steak, cut into strips
- 2 garlic cloves, minced
- 1 cup low-sodium beef broth
- ¼ cup reduced-sodium soy sauce
- 2 tablespoons balsamic vinegar
- 2 tablespoons brown sugar
- 15 ounces broccoli florets, fresh or frozen

Directions:

1. In a bowl, create a slurry by whisking together the cornstarch and water. Set aside.
2. Choose Sauté and add the olive oil. Once the oil is hot enough, add the steak, onion, and garlic; cook for about 3 minutes, stirring occasionally.
3. Press Cancel and add the broth, soy sauce, vinegar, and brown sugar; stir to combine. Using a wooden

spoon, remove any browned bits stuck to the bottom of the pot.

4. Secure the lid into place. Choose Pressure Cook or Manual; fix the pressure toHigh and the time to 10 minutes. Ensure the steam release knob is in the sealed position. Once done cooking, naturally release the pressure for 5 minutes, then quick release any remaining pressure.

5. Unlock and remove the lid. Add the broccoli florets.

6. Lock the lid into place again. Choose Pressure Cook or Manual; set the pressure to High and the time to 1 minute (3 minutes if using frozen florets). Ensure the steam release knob is in the sealed position. Once done cooking, quick release the pressure.

7. Open the lid. Choose Sauté. Use a slotted spoon to transfer the beef and vegetables to a serving bowl.

8. Whisk the cornstarch slurry into the liquid. Let it cook, uncovered, for 2 minutes or until the sauce starts to thicken. Press Cancel. Add the beef and vegetables into the pot and stir to combine.

9. Serve immediately, or place the beef and vegetables in a sealed container and refrigerate for up to 4 days or freeze for up to 2 months.

Nutrition: Calories – 321 Protein – 37 g. Fat – 14 g. Carbs – 10 g.

All-In-One Meatloaf with Mashed Potatoes

Preparation Time: 10 minutes

Cooking Time: 30 minutes

Servings: 8

Ingredients:

- 1 pound medium russet or Yukon Gold potatoes
- 1 cup low-sodium chicken broth
- 2 pounds 90% lean ground beef
- ½ medium yellow onion, chopped
- 2 garlic cloves, minced
- 1 egg
- 2 teaspoons Worcestershire sauce
- 1 teaspoon Dijon mustard
- 2 tablespoons unsalted butter
- 1 teaspoon fine sea salt
- ½ teaspoon freshly ground black pepper

Directions:

1. Place the potatoes and broth in the inner pot.
2. In a bowl, mix the ground beef, onion, garlic, egg, Worcestershire sauce, and mustard. Using your hands, combine the ingredients together thoroughly.

3. Form the meatloaf mixture into a loaf that will fit inside the inner pot.

4. Tear off a 2-foot piece of aluminum foil and fold it in half. Turn up the edges so it makes the shape of a square basket that will fit inside the inner pot. Place the meatloaf in the foil basket and place it on top of the potatoes.

5. Secure the lid into place. Choose Pressure Cook or Manual; fix the pressure toHigh and set to 30 minutes. Ensure the steam release knob is in the sealed position. Once done cooking, naturally release the pressure for 10 minutes, then quick release the remaining pressure.

6. Unlock and remove the lid. Carefully remove the meatloaf and the foil from the pot. Add the butter, salt, and pepper to the potatoes, then mash them to your liking with a potato masher or immersion blender.

7. Serve immediately, or place the meatloaf and mashed potatoes in separate airtight containers and refrigerate for up to 4 days or freeze for up to 2 months.

Nutrition: Calories – 286 Protein – 25 g. Fat – 14 g. Carbs – 12 g.

Hawaiian Pineapple Pork

Preparation Time: 10 minutes

Cooking Time: 15 minutes

Servings: 6

Ingredients:

- 2 tablespoons extra-virgin olive oil
- 2 lbs. pork loin, cut into 1-inch cubes
- 1 medium yellow onion, chopped
- 3 garlic cloves, minced
- 1 (20-ounce) can pineapple chunks in juice
- 2 red bell peppers, seeded and chopped
- ¼ cup reduced-sodium soy sauce
- 2 tablespoons brown sugar
- ¼ teaspoon chili powder

Directions:

1. Choose Sauté and add the olive oil to the inner container. Once the oil is hot enough, add the pork, onion, and garlic; sauté for 4 minutes, stirring occasionally to brown the pork on all sides.

2. Press Cancel and add the pineapple and its juice. Using a wooden spoon, remove any browned bits stuck to the bottom of the pot. Add the bell peppers, soy sauce, brown sugar, and chili powder. Stir to combine.

3. Secure the lid into place. Choose Pressure Cook or Manual; fix the pressure to High and the time to 10 minutes. Ensure the steam release knob is in the sealed position. Once done cooking, naturally release the pressure for 10 minutes, then quick release any remaining pressure.

4. Open the lid. Serve immediately, or place the pork and vegetables in an airtight container and refrigerate for up to 4 days.

Nutrition: Calories – 343 Protein – 30 g. Fat – 16 g. Carbs – 23 g.

PorkCarnitas

Preparation Time: 10 minutes

Cooking Time: 1 hour and 10 minutes

Servings: 6

Ingredients:

- 2 tablespoons extra-virgin olive oil
- 2 lbs. boneless pork roast, sliced into 2 or 3 pieces so it fits inside the pot
- 1 cup low-sodium chicken broth
- 1 teaspoon fine sea salt
- ½ teaspoon freshly ground black pepper
- 1 teaspoon ground cumin
- 1 teaspoon dried oregano
- 1 teaspoon chili powder
- ½ teaspoon garlic powder
- Juice of 2 limes

Directions:

1. Choose Sauté and add the olive oil to the inner pot. Once the oil is warm enough, addthe pork and brown it for 3 minutes. Turn the pork over and brown for 3 minutes more.

2. Press Cancel and pour in the broth. Using a wooden spoon, remove any browned bits stuck to the bottom

of the pot. Add the salt, pepper, cumin, oregano, chili powder, and garlic powder; stir to combine.

3. Secure the lid into place. Choose Pressure Cook or Manual; fix the pressure toHigh and the time to 60 minutes. Ensure the steam release knob is in the sealed position. Once done cooking, naturally release the pressure for 10 minutes, then quick release any remaining pressure.

4. Unlock and remove the lid. Stir in the lime juice. Using two forks, shred the pork. Serve immediately, or place the shredded pork in a sealed container and refrigerate for up to 4 days or freeze for up to 2 months.

Nutrition: Calories – 247 Protein – 35 g. Fat – 11 g. Carbs – 1 g.

Sweet and Sour Pork

Preparation Time: 15 minutes

Cooking Time: 18 minutes

Servings: 6

Ingredients:

- 2 tablespoons cornstarch
- ½ cup water
- 2 lbs. boneless pork shoulder, sliced into 1-inch pieces
- 1 tablespoon extra-virgin olive oil
- 1 medium yellow onion, chopped
- 2 garlic cloves, minced
- 1¼ cups freshly squeezed orange juice
- 2 tablespoons tomato paste
- ⅓ cup reduced-sodium soy sauce
- ¼ cup white wine vinegar
- ¼ cup honey
- 2 red bell peppers, seeded and sliced

Directions:

1. In a bowl, create a slurry by whisking together the cornstarch and water. Set aside.
2. Choose Sauté and add the olive oil. Once the oil is warm enough, addthe pork, onion, and garlic and sauté for 3 minutes, stirring occasionally.

---

3. Press Cancel and add the orange juice. Using a wooden spoon, remove any browned bits stuck to the bottom of the pot. Add the tomato paste, soy sauce, vinegar, honey, and bell peppers; stir to combine.

4. Secure the lid into place. Choose Pressure Cook or Manual; fix the pressure toHigh and the time to 8 minutes. Ensure the steam release knob is in the sealed position. Once done cooking, naturally release the pressure for 10 minutes, then quick release any remaining pressure.

5. Unlock and remove the lid. Select Sauté. Using a slotted spoon, take the pork and vegetables to a serving bowl.

6. Whisk the cornstarch slurry into the liquid and let it simmer, uncovered, for 2 minutes or until the sauce starts to thicken.

7. Place the pork and vegetables back in the pot and stir to combine. Serve immediately, or place the pork and vegetables in an airtight container and refrigerate for up to 4 days or freeze up to 2 months.

Nutrition: Calories – 332 Protein – 36 g. Fat – 9 g. Carbs – 27 g.

Tangy Vinegar Pork with Potatoes

Preparation Time: 15 minutes

Cooking Time: 35 minutes

Servings: 6

Ingredients:

- 2 tablespoons cornstarch
- ½ cup water
- 2 garlic cloves, minced
- 1 tablespoon extra-virgin olive oil
- 1¼ cups low-sodium chicken broth
- 2 lbs. boneless pork shoulder, sliced into 1-inch cubes
- ⅓ cup reduced-sodium soy sauce
- ¼ cup white wine vinegar
- 2 tablespoons honey
- ½ teaspoon freshly ground black pepper
- 1 pound white potatoes, cut into 1-inch cubes

Directions:

1. In a bowl, create a slurry by whisking together the cornstarch and water. Set aside.
2. Choose Sauté and add the olive oil. Once the oil is warm enough, addthe pork and garlic and sauté for 3 minutes, stirring occasionally.

3. Press Cancel and pour in the broth. Using a wooden spoon, remove any browned bits stuck to the bottom of the pot. Add the soy sauce, vinegar, honey, black pepper, and potatoes to the pot; stir to combine.

4. Secure the lid into place. Choose Pressure Cook or Manual; fix the pressure toHigh and the time to 25 minutes. Ensure the steam release knob is in the sealed position. Once done cooking, naturally release the pressure for 10 minutes, then quick release any remaining pressure.

5. Open the lid. Select Sauté. Using a slotted spoon, take the pork and potatoes to a serving plate.

6. Once the liquid in the pot is bubbling, whisk in the cornstarch slurry. Let the sauce simmer, uncovered, for about 2 minutes or until the sauce starts to thicken.

7. Put the pork and potatoes back to the pot and stir to combine. Serve immediately, or place the pork and potatoes in an airtight container and refrigerate for up to 4 days.

Nutrition: Calories – 318 Protein – 37 g. Fat – 8 g. Carbs – 22 g.

Polish Sausage with Sauerkraut

Preparation Time: 10 minutes

Cooking Time: 15 minutes

Servings: 6

Ingredients:

- 1 tablespoon extra-virgin olive oil
- 1 medium yellow onion, chopped
- 2 garlic cloves, minced
- 2 cups low-sodium chicken broth
- 1 (12-ounce) package fully cooked Polish sausage, cut into 1-inch-thick slices
- 1 (32-ounce) jar sauerkraut
- 1 apple, chopped
- 3 medium red potatoes, chopped into bite-size pieces

Directions:

1. Choose Sauté and add the olive oil to the inner pot. Once the oil is warm enough, addthe onion and garlic and sauté for 3 minutes, stirring occasionally.

2. Press Cancel and pour in the broth. Using a wooden spoon, remove any browned bits stuck to the bottom of the pot. Add the sausage slices, sauerkraut, apple, and potatoes; stir to combine.

3. Secure the lid into place. Choose Pressure Cook or Manual; fix the pressure toHigh and the time to 10 minutes. Ensure the steam release knob is in the sealed position. Once done cooking, naturally release the pressure for 10 minutes, then quick release any remaining pressure.

4. Unlock and remove the lid. Serve immediately, or place the sausages and veggies in an airtight container and refrigerate for up to 4 days.

Nutrition: Calories – 341 Protein – 12 g. Fat – 19 g. Carbs – 32 g.

Spicy Lamb Shoulder with Bulgur

Preparation Time: 10 minutes

Cooking Time: 1 hour and 5 minutes

Servings: 4

Ingredients:

- 25 oz lamb shoulder, cut into half
- 2 teaspoons chili pepper powder
- 5 tablespoons sunflower oil
- 1 tablespoon liquid smoke
- salt and pepper to taste
- 2 cups of bulgur
- 1 cup of water
- brown rice or steamed green beans for serving (optional)

Directions:

1. Rinse the bulgur numerous times and boil the water to cook the bulgur for about 20 minutes. Add 2 tbsp. sunflower oil when the bulgur is ready.
2. Fix your Air fryer to sauté mode and pour some oil to heat it up.
3. Add the lamb, salt, chili pepper powder and pepper, brown each side for 5 minutes until both sides are slightly browned.
4. Transfer them to a plate

5. Transfer the water and liquid smoke to the Air fryer and place the meat and spoon the bulgur.

6. Make sure to lock the lid and cook for1 hour on a HIGH pressure, then Naturally release the pressure over 10 minutes.

7. Transfer the lamb meat to the cutting board and shred using 2 forks. Portion the lamb into four plates and dollop each plate with the cooking liquid.

Nutrition: Calories – 374 Protein – 66 g. Fat – 73 g. Carbs – 269 g.

Beef Ribs with Lamb and Honey

Preparation Time: 10 minutes

Cooking Time: 1 hour

Servings: 4

Ingredients:

- 15 oz beef back ribs
- 15 oz lamb, diced
- 1 cup of cashews
- 2 tablespoons honey
- 1 teaspoon sesame oil
- 2 tablespoons soy sauce
- 1 teaspoon salt
- 1 teaspoon sugar
- 1 cup of water
- ½ cup of liquid smoke

Directions:

1. Preheat the oven to 240°-260° Fahrenheit and roast the cashews in the oven for 10 minutes until lcrispy and then let it cool completely. Then grind the cashews using a food processor or blender.

2. In a bowl, marinate the back ribs and lamb in honey. Then set the meat aside to marinate for a couple of hours at room temperature or place in the fridge overnight.

3. Add all the listed ingredients to the Air fryer.
4. Make sure to lock the lid and cook on MEAT/STEW mode for 60 minutes. Naturally release the pressure over 10 minutes. Portion the beef and lamb ribs into four plates and dollop each plate with the cooking liquid and soy sauce.

Nutrition: Calories – 367 Protein – 67 g. Fat – 74 g. Carbs – 268 g.

Lamb Sausages with Shrimps and Noodles

Preparation Time: 10 minutes

Cooking Time: 55 minutes

Servings: 4

Ingredients:

- 4 medium smoked lamb sausages, around 25 oz
- 1 cup of marinated small shrimps
- 1 cup of noodles
- 3 cups of water
- 1 medium onion, peeled and chopped
- 2 garlic cloves, minced
- 1 bouillon cube
- 2 tablespoons sunflower oil
- 1 teaspoon of cumin
- kosher salt, to taste
- black pepper, to taste

Directions:

1. Cut the sausages into cubes and fry them for 10 minutes.
2. Boil the water to cook the noodles for 10 minutes until half-cooked

3. Fix your Air fryer to sauté mode and pour in some sunflower oil. Add in the onions and garlic to sauté for 5 minutes until caramelized
4. Put your Pot to WARM mode and add in the remaining ingredients (except shrimps).
5. Close the lid and cook on a HIGH pressure for 35 minutes.
6. Naturally release the pressure over 10 minutes.
7. Portion the sausages and noodles into two bowls or mugs and dollop each bowl with the shrimps.

Nutrition: Calories – 285 Protein – 31 g. Fat – 32 g. Carbs – 61 g.

Spicy Lamb and Bean Rice

Preparation Time: 10 minutes

Cooking Time: 1 hour and 5 minutes

Servings: 4

Ingredients:

- 20 oz lamb, cubed
- 1 cup of brown rice
- 1 cup of red beans
- 3 cups of water
- 1 medium onion, peeled and chopped
- 1 yellow pepper, peeled and diced
- 2 garlic cloves, minced
- 1 bouillon cube
- 2 tablespoons sunflower oil
- 1 tablespoon chili powder
- ½ a teaspoon of cayenne pepper
- 1 teaspoon of cumin
- Salt and pepper

Directions:

1. Combine the chili powder, cumin, cayenne pepper, salt and pepper. Season the lamb with the spices and set the meat aside to marinate for a couple of hours at room temperature or place in the fridge overnight.

2. Soak the red beans in the warm water for overnight and then heat the water and boil the beans for around 10 minutes until half-cooked.

3. Rinse the brown rice several times and boil the water to cook the rice for 10 minutes until half-cooked.

4. Fix your Air fryer to sauté mode and put some sunflower oil. Add in the garlic and onions, to sauté for 5 minutes until caramelized.

5. Put your Air fryer to the WARM mode and add in the remaining ingredients (except the yellow pepper).

6. Make sure to lock the lid and cook for40 minutes on a HIGH pressure.

7. Naturally release the pressure over 10 minutes.

8. Portion the meat, beans and rice into four bowls or mugs and dollop each bowl with the yellow pepper cubes. Serve the lamb, beans and rice with the red wine.

Nutrition: Calories – 279 Protein – 25 g. Fat – 29 g. Carbs – 52 g.

Spicy Lamb with Garlic and Mustard

Preparation Time: 10 minutes

Cooking Time: 1 hour and 5 minutes

Servings: 4

Ingredients:

- 20 oz lamb
- 1 can of mustard
- 1/3 cup green pitted olives + 2 tablespoons brine
- 1 small red pepper, chopped
- 1 cup of water
- 8 garlic cloves, minced
- 2 tablespoons garlic powder
- 4 medium onions, peeled and chopped
- 1 and ¾ teaspoon garlic salt
- 5 tablespoons sunflower oil
- Black pepper to taste

Directions:

1. Combine the garlic, garlic powder, salt, black pepper, onion and pepper. Season the lamb with the spices and vegetables mix. Then toss the lamb in the mustard and set the lamb aside to marinate for a couple of hours at room temperature or place in the fridge overnight.

2. In a wok, heat the oil and fry the onions for around 10 minutes until clear and caramelized.

3. Add the lamb to the Pot and mix in the rest of the ingredients.

4. Make sure to lock the lid and cook the lamb on a HIGH pressure for 55 minutes.

5. Naturally release the pressure over 10 minutes. Slice the lamb and serve with the orange juice.

Nutrition: Calories – 386 Protein – 62 g. Fat – 84 g. Carbs – 262 g.

President Pork with Peanuts

Preparation Time: 10 minutes

Cooking Time: 50 minutes

Servings: 2

Ingredients:

- 25 oz pork
- 1 cup of peanuts
- 1 tablespoon Olive oil
- 1 teaspoon salt
- 1 teaspoon ground black pepper
- 1 teaspoon onion powder
- 1 teaspoon garlic powder
- 4 cups of beef broth
- fresh greenery

Directions:

1. Warm up the oven to 250°-270°F and roast the peanuts in the oven for 10 minutes until crispy and then set aside.

2. Place the pork into the Air fryer and season it well with the salt and pepper, mix well.

3. Add the oil and set the pot to sauté mode, sear each side of the beef for 10 minutes until crispy.

4. Pour the beef broth, onion powder, garlic powder, and mix well.

5. Make sure to lock the lid and cook on HIGH pressure for 40 minutes.

6. Once the timer goes off, naturally release the pressure over 10 minutes to open the lid.

7. Then cut the pork into cubes and portion it into two plates and top each plate with the fresh greenery and peanuts. Serve it with wine.

Nutrition: Calories – 384 Protein – 63 g. Fat – 85 g. Carbs – 264 g.

Pork with Apricots, Raisins and Pistachios

Preparation Time: 20 minutes

Cooking Time: 1 hour and 15 minutes

Servings: 2

Ingredients:

- 30 oz pork, ground
- 1 cup of pistachios
- 1 cup of dried apricots, chopped
- 1 cup of dried raisins, chopped
- 2 medium onions, peeled and chopped
- 6 cloves garlic, minced
- 2 teaspoons chili powder
- 3 teaspoons oregano
- 1 teaspoon cumin powder
- 5 tablespoons Olive oil
- 2 cups of tomatoes, chopped
- 2 cups of chicken broth
- 2 teaspoons nutmeg
- Salt and pepper to taste

Directions:

1. Wash and soak the raisins and the apricots in the warm water for 10 minutes and then set aside. Chop the apricots.
2. Mix in the salt, nutmeg, cumin, oregano, garlic, pistachios and black pepper. Flavor the pork with the spices mix. Then set the pork aside to marinate for a couple of hours at room temperature or place in the fridge overnight.
3. In a wok, heat the Olive oil and fry the chopped onions for around 10 minutes until clear and caramelized.
4. Put the air fryerto sauté mode and add in the Olive oil to heat it up.
5. Spoon the ground pork and stir for 5 minutes, breaking the meat.
6. Put the onions and sauté until fragrant, then spoon all the remaining ingredients and mix well.
7. Make sure to lock the lid and cook on a HIGH pressure for 50 minutes and then release the pressure over 10 minutes.
8. Serve with the white wine and enjoy!

Nutrition: Calories – 375 Protein – 58 g. Fat – 76 g. Carbs – 262 g.

Lamb and Zucchini

Preparation Time: 10 minutes

Cooking Time: 45 minutes

Servings: 3

Ingredients:

- 1 pound beef, sliced
- 1 medium zucchini, spiralized
- 1 cup of walnuts
- 3 tablespoons soy sauce
- 1 tablespoon dry basil
- 4 garlic cloves, minced
- 5 tablespoons Olive oil
- 2 tablespoons corn starch
- 1 cup of water
- 2 teaspoons salt
- black pepper, to taste
- fresh parsley

Directions:

1. Combine the garlic, salt and pepper. Toss the beef slices in the garlic mix. Then set the beef aside to marinate it for a couple of hours at room temperature or place in the fridge overnight.

2. Warm up the oven to 250°-270° Fahrenheit and roast the walnuts in the oven for 10 minutes until

lcrispy and then let it cool completely. Then grind the walnuts using a food processor or blender.

3. Add all the listed ingredients to your Pot and close the lid to cook on MEAT/STEW mode. Remember to set the timer to 35 minutes.

4. Release the pressure over 10 minutes. Serve with the fresh parsley and enjoy!

Nutrition: Calories – 368 Protein – 65 g. Fat – 78 g. Carbs – 267 g.

Spicy Rendang Lamb and Beef with Lemon

Preparation Time: 5 minutes

Cooking Time: 57 minutes

Servings: 4

Ingredients:

- 1 pound of skirt steak, cubed
- 20 oz lamb, diced
- 2 lemons, peeled and cubed
- 2 onions, peeled and chopped
- 1 tablespoon of ginger, minced
- 1 small jalapeno pepper, chopped
- 5 tablespoons sunflower oil
- 4 garlic cloves, minced
- 1 pack of rendang curry paste
- 1 cup of water

Directions:

1. In a bowl, mix in the onions, jalapeno pepper, garlic, ginger and rendang curry paste. Toss the steak and lamb in the spices and vegetables mix. Then set the meat aside for a couple of hours at room temperature or place in the fridge overnight.

2. Put your Air fryer to sauté mode and add in the sunflower oil and lemons.

3. Let the oil to heat up and add the meat and stir for about 2 minutes.
4. Pour a cup of water and close the lid to cook on a HIGH pressure for 55 minutes.
5. Open the lid and add in the lemon juice.

Nutrition: Calories – 369 Protein – 65 g. Fat – 79 g. Carbs – 263 g.

Lamb and Beef with Limes

Preparation Time: 25 minutes

Cooking Time: 1 hour and 5 minutes

Servings: 3

Ingredients:

- 20 oz lamb, cubed
- 15 oz beef, cubed
- 2 limes, halved
- 2 bacon slices
- 1 garlic clove, minced
- 1 medium onion, chopped
- 2 medium carrots, chopped
- 1 bunch of parsley, chopped
- 1 tablespoon thyme
- ½ a cup beef stock
- 1 large potato, cubed
- ½ a tablespoon olive oil
- Salt and pepper to taste

Directions:

1. In a bowl, mix in the garlic, parsley, salt and pepper. Toss the lamb and beef in the spices and sprinkle some lime juice over the meat. Then set the lamb and beef aside for a couple of hours at room temperature or place in the fridge overnight.

2. Put your pot to sauté mode and pour the oil, allow the oil to heat up.

3. Add the lamb and beef cubes and cook for 15 minutes.

4. Transfer the lamb and beef into a plate.

5. Add in the bacon and onion and sauté until translucent and caramelized. Then mix in all the vegetables and sauté for 20 minutes.

6. Add in the lamb and beef and all the remaining ingredients.

7. Make sure to lock the lid and cook for 30 minutes on a HIGH pressure.

8. Naturally release the pressure over 10 minutes.

9. Then portion the meat into three plates and top each plate with the cooked vegetables.

Nutrition: Calories – 387 Protein – 79 g. Fat – 88 g. Carbs – 289 g.

Lamb with Pineapple

Preparation Time: 15 minutes

Cooking Time: 55 minutes

Servings: 4

Ingredients:

- 25 oz lamb, ground
- ½ large onion, chopped
- 2 cups of pineapple, diced
- 1 garlic clove, minced
- 1 bay leaf
- 2 ounces tomato sauce
- 1 tablespoon olives, pitted
- 1 tablespoon cilantro, chopped
- ½ cup of water
- 2 teaspoon chili powder
- Salt and pepper, to taste

Directions:

1. Marinate the lamb in the salt, pepper and chili powder for a couple of hours at room temperature or place in the fridge overnight. Put the Air fryer to sauté mode and add in the pork. Break the lamb meat into pieces and cook for 10 minutes until browned.

   Add remaining ingredients and mix well.

---

2. Make sure to lock the lid and cook on HIGH pressure for 45 minutes.

3. Then portion the lamb into four plates. Serve with salad and brown rice.

Nutrition: Calories – 381 Protein – 71 g. Fat – 78 g. Carbs – 282 g.

POULTRY

Turkey Breasts

Preparation Time: 5 minutes

Cooking Time: 1 hour

Servings: 4

Ingredients:

- Boneless turkey breast – 3 lbs.
- Mayonnaise – ¼ cup
- Poultry seasoning – 2 tsps.
- Salt and pepper to taste
- Garlic powder – ½ tsp.

Directions:

1. Preheat the air fryer to 360F. Season the turkey with mayonnaise, seasoning, salt, garlic powder, and black pepper. Cook the turkey in the air fryer for 1 hour at 360F.

2. Turning after every 15 minutes. The turkey is done when it reaches 165F.

Nutrition: Calories 558; Carbs 1g; Fat 18g; Protein 98g

BBQ Chicken Breasts

Preparation Time: 5 minutes

Cooking Time: 15 minutes

Servings: 4

Ingredients:

- Boneless, skinless chicken breast – 4, about 6 oz. each
- BBQ seasoning – 2 tbsps.
- Cooking spray

Directions:

1. Rub the chicken with BBQ seasoning and marinate in the refrigerator for 45 minutes. Preheat the air fryer at 400F. Grease the basket with oil and place the chicken.
2. Then spray oil on top. Cook for 13 to 14 minutes. Flipping at the halfway mark. Serve.

Nutrition: Calories 131; Carbs 2g; Fat 3g; Protein 24g

Honey-Mustard Chicken Breasts

Preparation Time: 5 minutes

Cooking Time: 25 minutes

Servings: 6

Ingredients:

- Boneless, skinless chicken breasts – 6 (6-oz, each)
- Fresh rosemary – 2 tbsps. minced
- Honey – 3 tbsps.
- Dijon mustard – 1 tbsp.
- Salt and pepper to taste

Directions:

1. Combine the mustard, honey, pepper, rosemary and salt in a bowl. Rub the chicken with this mixture.

2. Grease the air fryer basket with oil. Air fry the chicken at 350F for 20 to 24 minutes or until the chicken reaches 165F. Serve.

Nutrition: Calories 236; Carbs 9.8g; Fat 5g; Protein 38g

Chicken Parmesan Wings

Preparation Time: 5 minutes

Cooking Time: 15 minutes

Servings: 4

Ingredients:

- Chicken wings – 2 lbs. cut into drumettes, pat dried
- Parmesan – ½ cup, plus 6 tbsps. grated
- Herbs de Provence – 1 tsp.
- Paprika – 1 tsp.
- Salt to taste

Directions:

1. Combine the parmesan, herbs, paprika, and salt in a bowl and rub the chicken with this mixture. Preheat the air fryer at 350F.
2. Grease the basket with cooking spray. Cook for 15 minutes. Flip once at the halfway mark. Garnish with parmesan and serve.

Nutrition: Calories 490; Carbs 1g; Fat 22g; Protein 72g

Air Fryer Chicken

Preparation Time: 5 minutes

Cooking Time: 30 minutes

Servings: 4

Ingredients:

- Chicken wings – 2 lbs.
- Salt and pepper to taste
- Cooking spray

Directions:

1. Flavor the chicken wings with salt and pepper. Grease the air fryer basket with cooking spray. Add chicken wings and cook at 400F for 35 minutes.
2. Flip 3 times during cooking for even cooking. Serve.

Nutrition: Calories 277; Carbs 1g; Fat 8g; Protein 50g

Whole Chicken

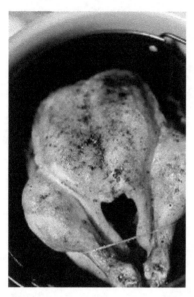

Preparation Time: 5 minutes

Cooking Time: 40 minutes

Servings: 6

Ingredients:

- Whole chicken – 1 (2 ½ pounds) washed and pat dried
- Dry rub – 2 tbsps.
- Salt – 1 tsp.
- Cooking spray

Directions:

1. Preheat the air fryer at 350F. Rub the dry rub on the chicken. Then rub with salt. Cook it at 350°F for 45

minutes. After 30 minutes, flip the chicken and finish cooking.

2. Chicken is done when it reaches 165F.

Nutrition: Calories 412; Carbs 1g; Fat 28g; Protein 35g

Honey Duck Breasts

Preparation Time: 5 minutes

Cooking Time: 25 minutes

Servings: 2

Ingredients:

- Smoked duck breast – 1, halved
- Honey – 1 tsp.
- Tomato paste – 1 tsp.
- Mustard – 1 tbsp.
- Apple vinegar – ½ tsp.

Directions:

1. Mix tomato paste, honey, mustard, and vinegar in a bowl. Whisk well. Add duck breast pieces and coat well. Cook in the air fryer at 370F for 15 minutes.

2. Remove the duck breast from the air fryer and add to the honey mixture. Coat again. Cook again at 370F for 6 minutes. Serve.

Nutrition:

Calories 274; Carbs 22g; Fat 11g; Protein 13g

Creamy Coconut Chicken

Preparation Time: 5 minutes

Cooking Time: 20 minutes

Servings: 4

Ingredients:

- Big chicken legs – 4
- Turmeric powder – 5 tsps.
- Ginger – 2 tbsps. grated
- Salt and black pepper to taste
- Coconut cream – 4 tbsps.

Directions:

1. In a bowl, mix salt, pepper, ginger, turmeric, and cream. Whisk. Add chicken pieces, coat and marinate for 2 hours.
2. Transfer chicken to the preheated air fryer and cook at 370F for 25 minutes. Serve.

Nutrition: Calories 300; Carbs 22g; Fat 4g; Protein 20g

Buffalo Chicken Tenders

Preparation Time: 5 minutes

Cooking Time: 20 minutes

Servings: 4

Ingredients:

- Boneless, skinless chicken tenders – 1 pound
- Hot sauce – ¼ cup
- Pork rinds – 1 ½ ounces, finely ground
- Chili powder – 1 tsp.
- Garlic powder – 1 tsp.

Directions:

1. Put the chicken breasts in a bowl and pour hot sauce over them. Toss to coat. Mix ground pork rinds, chili powder and garlic powder in another bowl.
2. Place each tender in the ground pork rinds, and coat well. With wet hands, press down the pork rinds into

the chicken. Place the tender in a single layer into the air fryer basket. Cook at 375F for 20 minutes. Flip once. Serve.

Nutrition: Calories 160; Carbs 0.6g; Fat 4.4g; Protein 27.3g

Teriyaki Wings

Preparation Time: 5 minutes

Cooking Time: 20 minutes

Servings: 4

Ingredients:

- Chicken wings – 2 pounds
- Teriyaki sauce – ½ cup
- Minced garlic – 2 tsp.
- Ground ginger - ¼ tsp.
- Baking powder – 2 tsp.

Directions:

1. Except for the baking powder, place all ingredients in a bowl and marinate for 1 hour in the refrigerator. Place wings into the air fryer basket and sprinkle with baking powder.
2. Gently rub into wings. Cook at 400F for 25 minutes. Shake the basket two- or three-times during cooking. Serve.

Nutrition: Calories 446; Carbs 3.1g; Fat 29.8g; Protein 41.8g

CONCLUSION

Air fryers are a relatively new piece of kitchen gadgetry. They are used by individuals who want to cook healthy foods using less oil and less fat then their conventional counterparts.

In addition to being a healthier alternative to deep frying, air fryers are also fun to use. Air-frying not only produces lots of fun and tasty food, it also saves you time and money. You can cook without the need of a griddle or a stovetop, which frees up your kitchen so you can focus on eating more healthy foods!

It is important to have an air fryer that is up to par. If you want an air fryer that will last for years, make sure that you buy an durable one. To help you choose the right air fryer for you, we have compiled a list of the best air fried ovens!

The Airfryer has several seating options. The four different versions include:

Small Seating–The size of the seating area is 13.5" x 8.5" x 9.5".

Medium Seating–The size of the seating area is 20" x 12".

Large Seating–The size of the seating area is 23" x 15".

Extra Large Seating–The size is 32" X 21". The extra large seat could accommodate up to 8 pieces. A small, medium or large fryer is included with every air fryer and can be purchased separately. The only part that may need to be purchased separately is a colander for the basket which will hold up to 16 cups depending on the size of the basket that you are using. There are no other accessories required for the air fryer: please see the specifications on this page for further details.

What's happening to our restaurant food? The answer is rather simple. We are over-cooking and over-frying foods, and most of it is for the wrong reasons.

Nobody wants to eat overcooked, undercooked, or under-salted food. Restaurant owners are turning away good customers in the name of profit.

That's not our fault. It's up to the professional chefs to do a better job with their cooking skills.

We use our Air Fryers to cook foods that don't require cooking at all. We use them to cook and heat our foods in such a way that they're ready to eat right out of the air fryer. There's no need for you to heat up your kitchen with a conventional oven or stove, just put the food in and let it finish fully. You'll be amazed at how delicious your foods can taste when you use an Air Fryer!

Today's busy lifestyle often leaves us with little time to cook. For those of you who don't have time to cook, but still need your food, the air fryer is for you.

An air fryer is an appliance that cooks food by circulating hot air over it. The circulating air causes the food to slowly cook within a sealed container while removing excess oil and fat from the food. By sealing the food in a hermetic chamber during cooking, no additional oil is released into the air. This is important because it prevents the flavor of the food from being compromised. The result is a fast and easy way to prepare delicious meals without having to use any grease or oils while eroding your pantry of oils.

In this air fryer cookbook, we will teach you how to use your air fryer most effectively and how to avoid common mistakes. From learning how to clean and maintain your air fryer to finding creative recipes, this guide will help you get the most out of your air fryer today

CPSIA information can be obtained
at www.ICGtesting.com
Printed in the USA
BVHW070819070521
606649BV00002B/406